£3.50

Contents

© 1986 GRANDREAMS LIMITED

Edited by *John Barraclough;* Layout & design by *Nigel
I. Money;* Written by *Tony Lynch;* All photographs
supplied by and are copyright *Photographers International.*
Printed in Holland. ISBN 0 86227 401 X

Published by
GRANDREAMS LIMITED,
Jadwin House, 205/211 Kentish Town Road,
London NW5 2JU

iana, Princess of Wales, is without doubt the most famous woman of the 'eighties.

Since her somewhat sudden appearance on the royal scene in 1980 (as Lady Diana Spencer, a rather shy nineteen year-old kindergarten teacher) she has grown in poise and stature and has carved a unique niche of her very own within the history of the British Royal Family.

Millions of words have been written about her in newspapers, magazines and books. She has been dubbed 'The Superstar Princess', 'The Fairytale Princess', 'Princess Wonderful' and a whole host of other superlatives besides.

She is certainly the most photographed woman in the world. Wherever she goes, a camera is sure to follow. Indeed, the photographers love her for her photogenic qualities — classical beauty, a tall slim figure, beautiful blue eyes, an English rose complexion, impeccably styled hair and, of course, a highly developed sense of fashion.

The Princess of Wales always looks good in pictures — and this Grandreams Special celebrates the fact with some of the finest photographs ever taken of her.

As usual, cameras were on hand when the Prince and Princess danced together at the Southern Cross Ball in Melbourne, in October 1985. The choice of melody that evening was entirely appropriate — it was Stevie Wonder's great up-tempo hit **"Isn't She Lovely"**. The sentiments expressed by that song seem to sum up everyone's feelings about Diana, Princess of Wales . . .

The Princess of Wales at her most beguiling as she dances with Prince Charles at the Southern Cross Ball in Melbourne. Many people believe that the great revival in interest in the British Royal Family began with Diana's arrival on the scene.

"Isn't She Lovely"

The Story of a Princess

Childhood & Schooldays

The Honourable Diana Frances Spencer — the girl destined to become the Princess of Wales — was born on July 1 1961, at Park House, Sandringham, Norfolk.

She was the third daughter born to the then Viscount and Viscountess Althorp. The Viscount, Edward John, was a former equerry to King George VI and he later performed the same service for Queen Elizabeth II. His wife, Frances Ruth, was the daughter of Lady Fermoy a lady-in-waiting to the Queen Mother. Diana's elder sisters were Sarah, born in 1955, and Jane, born in 1957. A brother, Charles, would be born in 1964.

Park House stands on Sandringham's world famous royal estate. Since the time of Queen Victoria it has been the home of courtiers to the Royal Family. It was here, as a very young girl, that the Honourable Diana Spencer first saw Prince Charles — although in later years neither could recall the meeting.

The Prince's brothers, Andrew and Edward, as well as other young members of the Royal Family, often visited Park House when they were staying at Sandringham. The attraction there was a large heated swimming pool, a luxury which the main house did not possess.

It was in this distinctly 'royal' environment that the young Diana Spencer spent her childhood years. As an infant she was always known as a tender-hearted child who loved cuddly toys and small, furry animals.

At the age of six a time of great sadness entered her life when her parents separated and later divorced.

The Spencer children remained in the custody of their father, but they often went to stay with their mother, occasionally spending holidays with her in Scotland.

At first young Diana's education was provided by her first governess, Gertrude Allen, in the schoolroom at Park House. 'Ally', as she was known, had also taught Diana's mother when she was a child.

In 1968, when she was seven, the future Princess began to attend Silfield, a private day school in nearby King's Lynn. Here, it was noted that she had good handwriting, was a good reader and had an extremely cheerful personality.

Young Diana stayed at Silfield for two years. Then she became a boarder at Riddlesworth Hall, a girls preparatory school near Diss, some thirty miles away from Sandringham. Again she was

a well-liked and very capable pupil who proved to be particularly good at games and swimming.

To help teach them the meaning of responsibility, the girls at Riddlesworth Hall were encouraged to keep pets, and a special Pets' Corner was provided by the school for just that purpose. Diana kept a prize winning guinea pig called 'Peanuts'.

At the age of twelve she changed schools yet again — this time travelling many miles from home, to West Heath, an exclusive boarding school for girls, near Sevenoaks in Kent.

During her four years at West Heath, the youthful Diana continued to excel at games and swimming, winning several cups for water sports. She loved tennis, too, and was usually

taken by her mother to the first Saturday of the Wimbledon Championships. She also became a keen dancer, and for a while wanted to become a ballerina — an ambition which she literally *grew* out of.

Appropriately enough her favourite academic subject was History.

During this time she also developed a caring interest in the elderly and in handicapped children — an interest which led to her being given a Special Award by the school in her final term.

In 1975 the *Honourable* Diana Spencer became *Lady* Diana Spencer when her father inherited the title of Earl Spencer upon the death of his father. The family left the relative cosiness of Park House and moved into their

ancestral home, Althorp — a 75-roomed stately mansion near Great Brington in Northamptonshire.

In July of the following year the Earl remarried. His new wife was Raine, former Countess of Dartmouth. She was the rather flamboyant daughter of the best-selling romantic novelist Barbara Cartland.

Lady Diana and her brother and sisters now had a stepmother. Diana, being the youngest of the girls, was able to adjust more easily than her sisters to the presence of this new figure of authority in their lives. (Their mother had also remarried, in 1969, to Peter Shand Kydd, a businessman and farmer with land in Britain and Australia.)

In December 1977 Lady Diana went off to Switzerland

where she was to attend a finishing school — the Institut Alpin Videmanette at the Chateau d'Oex, near Gstaad.

With her she took one very special memory, for just a few weeks earlier, the family at Althorp had had a very important guest of honour — none other than the Prince of Wales himself.

Although she couldn't possibly know it, Lady Diana had met her future husband, for the first time that either of them can recall. And the meeting had taken place in the middle of a freshly ploughed field!

She thought him 'pretty amazing'. He thought she was '. . . jolly and amusing and attractive . . .' That was all there was to it at the time, and they both went on their separate ways.

Although she had enrolled at the Institut Alpin Videmanette for three months, Lady Diana quickly found herself suffering all the agonies of homesickness. Consequently she came home to England after just six weeks and did not return to the finishing school.

Meanwhile, the name of her eldest sister, Sarah, had been romantically linked with that of the Prince of Wales. This was, in fact, just one in a long line of speculative stories which had appeared in the press.

In recent years Fleet Street had devoted many column inches in attempting to answer the burning question: 'Who Will Become the Future Wife of the Future King of England?' This particular relationship ended when Lady Sarah gave an interview to a women's magazine in which she described her friendship with Prince Charles as "totally platonic". (Lady Sarah married Neil McCorquodale in 1980.)

Lady Diana, thinking about a possible career, had decided that she wanted to work with children.

She moved to London and became a student teacher at a dance studio in Brompton Road where her duties consisted mainly of shepherding tiny tots and other children about the place.

At first she lived at her mother's house in Cadogan Place, Chelsea. Then, shortly after her eighteenth birthday in July 1979, she moved into

a home of her own — a large well-appointed flat in Coleherne Court, off Old Brompton Road in South Kensington. She shared this flat with three other young women, Ann Bolton, Virginia Pitman and Caroline Pride.

After a summer holiday spent with her mother in Scotland, Lady Diana returned to London to begin a new job as an assistant teacher at the Young England Kindergarten in St. George's Square, Pimlico.

Meanwhile her romance with Prince Charles was beginning to blossom — in secret.

The Prince invited her to watch him play polo at Cowdray in July 1980, and in September of that year she was his guest at Balmoral. And it was there, on the banks of the River Dee, where Diana was watching Prince Charles fishing, that she was first spotted by a wily reporter and two press photographers.

Lady Diana smiles shyly at the camera as she leaves the Ritz Hotel in London, following Princess Margaret's 50th birthday party held in November 1980.

Below: Keeping her thoughts to herself, the young kindergarten teacher carries on with her work. Wherever she went a camera was sure to follow. *Right:* 'Shy Di' was always a problem for the photographers, as she seldom looked up. This was one solution! Coleherne Court is seen in the background. *Below, right:* Lady Diana with pupils of the Young England Kindergarten. She was a great favourite with the children there.

Lady Diana was well aware of their presence for she had observed them, with the aid of a make-up mirror, while hiding behind a tree.

Suddenly, with a headscarf and a cap hiding her features, she strode forward and disappeared over the brow of the nearest hill, away from the prying lenses.

During the following week the Fleet Street floodgates opened — and a pretty, shy and unknown kindergarten teacher suddenly found herself at the centre of the biggest news story of the day.

The same wily reporter, back from Scotland, quickly discovered where she lived. The flat at Coleherne Court was besieged at all hours by 'doorstepping' photographers and reporters, all patiently waiting for the briefest appearance of Lady Diana.

She, in turn, was always polite and courteous to the ladies and gentlemen of the press. But she never gave even so much as a hint of confirmation to the rumours of romance.

The Young England Kindergarten also became a centre of media attention. In one celebrated incident, in September 1980, Lady Diana agreed to be photographed in the sunshine in St. George's Square, with two of the toddlers in her care. Thanks to some skilful Fleet Street manipulation she appeared in the next day's papers wearing a seemingly 'see-through' dress, back-lit by the rays of the sun.

While Lady Diana was embarrassed and a little annoyed by these pictures, Prince Charles saw the amusing side of things. A few days later he is reported to have told her: "I knew your legs were good. But I didn't realise they were that spectacular!"

Having learned this rather tough lesson, Lady Diana became a lot more wary in her dealings with the media. Future meetings with the Prince would be subject to the utmost secrecy and discretion.

These tactics worked very successfully, for Prince Charles and Lady Diana were not seen in the same place in public until some four weeks later. The venue was a race meeting at Ludlow in Shropshire at which the Prince rode his own horse, Allibar, in a race for amateur riders. But even here the couple were not actually seen together.

Their meetings continued, away from the constant glare of the publicity machine. The Prince gave Lady Diana a

conducted tour of Highgrove House, the Georgian mansion he had recently purchased, near Tetbury in Gloucestershire.

The couple were guests at Princess Margaret's 50th birthday party, held at London's Ritz Hotel in November 1980. Later that same month Lady Diana was at Sandringham for Prince Charles' 32nd birthday celebrations.

That autumn Prince Charles left Britain for an official tour of India and Nepal. This left Lady Diana to contend with the ever-mounting pressure from the media. Her mother wrote an indignant letter to The Times requesting that the reporters and photographers should leave Diana alone — but all to no avail. Everywhere she went, the cameras were sure to follow.

Prince Charles spent New Year 1981 at Klosters in Switzerland. Upon his return to England at the beginning of February, he invited Lady Diana to dine with him at Buckingham Palace. After the meal he asked her to marry him.

Outside of the Royal Family and the Spencer family, Diana's flatmates at Coleherne Court were among the first to hear the news. They of course were overjoyed at the good tidings — but, naturally, they were sworn to secrecy.

Shortly afterwards Lady Diana travelled to the other side of the world, to spend a short holiday with her mother and her stepfather on their sheep farm at Murrumbidgee in Australia.

Even here she was

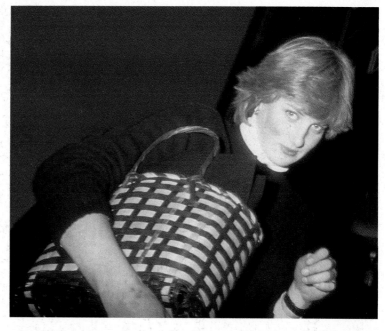

constantly pestered by the media. But the security arrangements were so efficient that Prince Charles himself encountered great difficulty when attempting to speak to his fiancée by telephone!

An Announcement is made

Main picture: *Photo-call with Prince Charles at Balmoral after the engagement announcement had been made.* Right, above: *The Prince and his fiancée arrive for a gala evening at the Goldsmith's Hall in London. This was Diana's first public engagement following the engagement. She is wearing 'The Dress That Stole the Show!'* Right, below: *Lady Diana with Prince Charles and Princess Margaret at the wedding of Nicholas Soames and Catherine Wetherall. The Prince was best man.*

ack in London on Tuesday February 24, at 11a.m. precisely, the Lord Chamberlain, head of the royal household, made an announcement to guests gathered for an Investiture ceremony at Buckingham Palace.

He said: "It is with the greatest pleasure that the Queen and the Duke of Edinburgh announce the betrothal of their beloved son, the Prince of Wales, to Lady Diana Spencer, daughter of the Earl Spencer and the Honourable Mrs Shand Kydd."

From the moment that the announcement was made public, the nation went wild with wedding fever. It was good news for a change, and proved to be just the tonic that Britain needed.

Crowds of well-wishers gathered outside Buckingham Palace, and the band of the Coldstream Guards gave endless renditions of the hit tune **'Congratulations'**.

Everyone was happy.

During a photo-call at Buckingham Palace, Lady Diana proudly displayed her engagement ring — a magnificent sapphire surrounded by fourteen diamonds on a bed of platinum. It had been purchased from Garrards, the Crown Jewellers, at a cost of over £28,000.

With her husband-to-be by her side, Lady Diana gave her first media interview, in which she said: "It is always nice when there are two of you and there's someone

there to help you.".

From now on, if such a thing were possible, she would be scrutinised even more closely by TV, radio, newspapers and magazines from all over the world.

For Lady Diana Spencer, life would never be the same again.

19

The Royal Wedding Day was duly named — July 29 1981 — and the venue for the ceremony was announced as St. Paul's Cathedral. This was the choice of both Prince Charles and Lady Diana and it surprised many commentators who had expected the couple to follow royal tradition and marry at Westminster Cathedral.

On March 9 Lady Diana, with her fiancé by her side, attended her first official public engagement — a charity gala evening at the Goldsmiths' Hall in London.

As expected the future Princess of Wales stole the show — but no-one expected it to happen in so spectacular a fashion. She wore a simply stunning black taffeta strapless gown which managed to upstage everything else that evening.

Next day it was revealed that the dress had been designed by David and Elizabeth Emanuel, and that they had been commissioned to design Lady Diana's wedding gown.

With barely five months between the engagement announcement and the wedding day, the Emanuels were not the only ones to get busy.

Indeed, a whole 'royal wedding industry' sprang up almost overnight. Any amount of red, white and blue souvenirs were soon available. These ranged from decorated mugs, plates, cups and saucers, serviettes, toast racks, tea cosies and tea towels — to more immediate items such as plastic Union Jacks, postcards, balloons, hats, T-shirts and even cut-out models of the royal couple able to 'wave' regally from the side windows of a car!

An Ode to the royal couple was composed by the then Poet Laureate, Sir John Betjeman, and a new portrait of Lady Diana — painted by Bryan Organ — was unveiled at the National Portrait Gallery where it now hangs alongside the same artist's portrait of Prince Charles.

The wedding ring was made of Welsh gold from the same nugget used for the wedding rings of the Queen Mother, the Queen, Princess Margaret and Princess Anne.

Countdown to a Royal Wedding

The splendid five-tier wedding cake was baked, iced, and laced with rum by the Royal Navy at Chatham, and the special wedding licence was delicately inscribed by an expert calligrapher in Wiltshire.

And of course it was a very busy time for Prince Charles and Lady Diana, too.

After a tearful parting from each other at London airport, the Prince left for a five-week tour of Australia, New Zealand and Canada.

Upon his return the couple attended several more official engagements together. These included two very successful days of

'royal walkabouts', one of which took place in Tetbury, Gloucestershire, just a mile or so from Highgrove House their future home together.

There were also dinners and state banquets to attend, given in honour of visiting dignitaries. And the couple visited Princess Anne in hospital after the birth of her daughter, Zara, on May 15.

Prince Charles was best-man at the wedding of his friend Nicholas Soames to Catherine Wetherall, held at St. Margaret's, Westminster. There were visits for Lady Diana to the racing at Ascot, the Wimbledon tennis championships, and to watch her fiancé playing polo at Windsor.

And of course there were several rehearsals for the great day itself — and a private meeting with Robert Runcie, the Archbishop of Canterbury, who would perform the ceremony.

Slowly but surely July 29 drew nearer and nearer.

On Sunday July 26 many thousands of people trod the 'royal route' for themselves — from Buckingham Palace, along The Mall, through the south side of Trafalgar Square, into the Strand, through the Aldwych, along Fleet Street, up Ludgate Hill and to St. Paul's Cathedral itself.

Every building along the way had been spruced-up for the great occasion, and many of them were already bedecked with flags and bunting. It was estimated on that pre-wedding Sunday that almost 15,000 visitors entered the Cathedral.

At several spots along the route people in little encampments of deck chairs and camping stoves and sleeping bags were already staking their claim to a good view of the wedding procession.

Street parties sprang up all over the country. The biggest one was held in London's Oxford Street, entertaining thousands of deprived children who sat down at over 800 tables to a feast of hamburgers, cakes, jelly, ice cream and lemonade.

The excitement continued to grow throughout Monday and Tuesday with more red, white and blue appearing on the streets of London, along with more and more keen spectators.

Shortly after 10 p.m. on Tuesday, Prince Charles lit the first of 101 beacons which would blaze on high ground all over the country.

A magnificent firework display was lit in Hyde Park, to the accompaniment of military music and cannon fire. It was a splendid spectacle seen by many thousands of people in the park, and by many millions more on TV.

Lady Diana spent the eve of her wedding at Clarence House, home of the Queen Mother. There she retired early to bed.

Outside, the night fell cool and dry over London. And the crowds along the royal route thickened and grew and waited for morning.

29th July, 1981.
A Day to Remember

Above: People came from all over the world to watch the wedding. This happy New Zealander was determined to enjoy a right royal occasion. *Right:* A tiny part of the crowd on July 29 1981. Simple periscopes made of cardboard and cheap mirrors were selling for $1 each, but they did the trick even though they fell apart afterwards!

he wedding day dawned. The patiently waiting crowd began to stir from an uncomfortable night, spent in sleeping bags, deckchairs, tents, or just plain blankets or coats spread on the ground. The royal route, lined with policemen, was closed off in the early hours — and any official car, horse or pedestrian that appeared along it was given a rousing, good-natured cheer by the spectators.

More and more people joined the throng as the day wore on until it was estimated that a million or more lined the route.

Inside Clarence House Lady Diana rose early to prepare for her great day. Her hair was coiffured by her favourite stylist Kevin Shanley. Her make-up and manicure was applied by the famous make-up artist Barbara Daly.

Lady Diana then put on the magnificent wedding dress, designed and made by the Emanuels. As a token of good luck they sewed the final stitches while the bride was wearing the dress. The Emanuels' creation,

kept under wraps for so long, was made from forty-four yards of ivory-coloured silk taffeta, hand-embroidered with pearls and mother-of-pearl sequins, and edged with lace. The train was some twenty-five feet long, and the veil was secured by the diamond-encrusted Spencer Tiara. As an insurance against disaster, two copies of the dress stood by — just in case!

Left: The newly-weds emerge from St. Paul's Cathedral to the tumultuous cheers of the crowd. The wedding day was a tremendous occasion full of pomp and ceremony. *Above:* The wedding ceremony inside St. Paul's Cathedral. Members of the Royal Family look on with pride.

Also preparing inside Clarence House were the five bridesmaids (also wearing dresses by the Emanuels) and the two page boys dressed in the uniforms of Victorian Naval Cadets.

At 10.05 a.m. the wedding procession set out from Buckingham Palace.

The crowd was in for a right royal treat as the state coaches, each accompanied by a horse-borne escort, carried members of the Royal Family towards St. Paul's, nearly two miles away.

The order of the cavalcade was as follows: The Duke and Duchess of Kent, Prince and Princess Michael of Kent, Princess Alexandra and the Honourable Angus Ogilvy, the Duke and Duchess of Gloucester, Princess Anne and Captain Mark Phillips, Princess Margaret, the Queen Mother and Prince Edward, and the Queen and Prince Philip.

Then came the bridegroom, in the full dress uniform of a Navy Commander, complete with a blue Garter sash. Prince Charles was accompanied by Prince Andrew, who was to act as a 'supporter' along with Prince Edward. Among Andrew's most important tasks of the day was the carrying of the wedding ring.

At 10.30 Lady Diana stepped into the fabulous Glass Coach to sit beside her proud father, Earl Spencer, who had only recently recovered from a serious illness.

The coach clattered into The Mall to tumultuous applause and cheering, by far the loudest of the day so far. People craned their necks to catch a glimpse of the beautiful bride, and of that mysterious dress.

For almost half an hour the Glass Coach made its way along the royal route on a red, white and blue sea of affection. Shortly before

other Kings, Queens, Princes, Princesses, Dukes and Duchesses as well as more than 160 top-ranking government officials from all over the world. Other guests included Prince Charles' favourite comedian, Spike Milligan, Lady Diana's ex-flatmates from Coleherne Court, some of her old schoolfriends and members of staff from Althorp — all of them as pleased as punch. These people, together with the remaining guests and around 700 million TV viewers around the world, then proceeded to watch the very stirring ceremony performed by the Archbishop of Canterbury. The service was accompanied by some splendid music including the Trumpet Voluntary *and an aria from* Samson *sung by the great opera star Kiri Te Kanawa.*
Both partners fluffed their lines during the making of their vows. She *actually got*

Left: On the royal route back to Buckingham Palace. The new Princess of Wales waves to the crowd with her husband by her side.
Below: Romance is in the air as the Prince kisses the hand of his Princess, on the balcony of Buckingham Palace.

eleven o'clock it came to a halt outside St. Paul's, and Lady Diana stepped out revealing for the first time the magnificent splendour of that dress — an instant hit with everyone who saw it. Before Diana entered the cathedral her wedding train was arranged behind her by two of the bridesmaids. And then came the long, long walk along the aisle, a distance of more than 200 metres, to the dais where her husband-to-be awaited her. Watching these moments inside the cathedral were over 2,500 wedding guests. Apart from the British Royal Family there were numerous

his christian names in the wrong order, while he missed out the word 'worldly' and promised to share all her own goods with her! They both said "I will" and the Archbishop pronounced them to be man and wife. As these words were heard all over the world, a tumultuous cheer rang out through the streets of London and a magnificent peal of bells was heard all over the city. Lady Diana was now Diana, Princess of Wales.

In the open landau that had carried Prince Charles and Prince Andrew to the

cathedral, the newly-weds rode back along the royal route to Buckingham Palace. The remainder of the Royal Family followed in their respective coaches. Every inch of the way was crammed with happy, smiling faces, and flags and flowers in every shade of red, white and blue.

When the procession was over, the crowds were allowed onto the route. A sea of people poured into The Mall and flowed towards the Palace to await the appearance of the royal couple on the balcony there.

Meanwhile, inside the

Palace, the famous photographer Lord Lichfield was taking the official wedding photos — with the aid of a referee's whistle to help him gain the attention of everyone in the group! After the photo-session the Prince and his new Princess stepped out onto the balcony to greet the crowds. The rest of the family, led by the Queen, followed them. In all they made four appearances, during the last of which the Prince and Princess kissed each other. At that, the crowd gave their loudest cheer of the day. A wedding breakfast

followed — it was actually a three-course lunch — after which Prince Charles cut the Navy's magnificent cake with his ceremonial sword. An hour later the Prince and Princess, together with the Queen and Prince Philip, made a further, unscheduled, appearance on the balcony — and once again the crowd went wild with delight. In the afternoon the royal couple left the Palace in their open landau en route for Waterloo Station. As at all good weddings the going-away transport had been tampered with — this one by Prince Andrew and Prince Edward. The two brothers had bedecked the coach with silver balloons and had hung a handwritten 'Just Married' sign on the back!

On Platform 12 at Waterloo the newly-weds were greeted by British Rail officials together with the Comptroller of the Queen and the Lord Chamberlain. These were the two men who had been responsible for the smooth running of the wedding day. In a spontaneous gesture of thanks Diana kissed them both.

The special three-coach Royal Train waited. It was ready to take the Prince and Princess on the 80-mile journey to Romsey in Hampshire, where the honeymoon would begin at Broadlands, the home of Lord Romsey.

During his wedding address Robert Runcie, the Archbishop of Canterbury had said: "Here is the stuff of which fairy tales are made." And indeed that whole day, July 29 1981, was for many touched by a kind of magic.

The Royal Honeymoon

he newly-weds left Broadlands on Saturday August 1 1981, and were taken by limousine to nearby Eastleigh airport. There they boarded an RAF Andover of The Queen's Flight. The 'plane, piloted by Prince Charles, then took-off for Gibraltar where the honeymooners were to join the royal yacht *Britannia*.

The Prince and Princess were welcomed by the people of Gibraltar with almost as much enthusiasm as they had seen on their wedding day in London.

It seemed that the whole of the tiny island was bedecked in red, white and blue bunting. In fact all the Union Jacks had sold out and many people were waving the red, white and blue of the French tricolour!

After a brief tour of the famous Rock of Gibraltar and a reception on board *Britannia*, the royal couple set sail.

But where was she heading? That was the burning question posed by the media. All details of the honeymoon itinerary had been kept a secret from them.

In fact, *Britannia* sailed along the coast

of Algeria and then took in a spot of island hopping in the lovely Greek isles. Her first official port of call was Port Said in Egypt, where the royal couple were formally welcomed by the late President Sadat and his wife.

The final days of the honeymoon cruise were spent on the Red Sea — without a camera in sight.

The newly-weds left *Britannia* and flew directly from Hurghada in south-eastern Egypt to Lossiemouth in Scotland. From there they travelled on to Balmoral where the rest of the Royal Family welcomed them back.

Later in the week the couple posed happily for the photographers who had attempted to trail them all around the Mediterranean. Ironically, this photo-call took place on the banks of the River Dee where Diana had first been spotted by that wily reporter and his photographers, some eleven months earlier.

The New Princess of Wales

By the end of October the honeymoon was over and the new Princess of Wales prepared for her royal duties.

Her first official engagement was to be a three-day, 400 mile whistle-stop tour of Wales in the company of her husband.

Diana was the first Princess of Wales for almost eighty years, and the people were more than happy to celebrate the fact — especially when she arrived in Caernarfon dressed in the Welsh national colours of red and green.

It was a bitterly cold day and the Princess won the hearts of the crowd by sympathising with them for having waited for so long to see her. Everyone, it seemed, wanted to shake her by the hand.

Whilst in Caernarfon the royal couple visited the Castle where, in 1969, Prince Charles had received his Investiture as Prince of Wales. Here a choir of school children, shivering with the cold, sang traditional Welsh songs in honour of the visitors.

The remaining two days of the tour were conducted in torrential rain. But the weather did little to dampen the enthusiasm of the Welsh well-wishers as the royal motorcade progressed on its journey. In fact, they adored their Princess all the more when she showed that she was not afraid of a drop of rain.

The Princess concluded the tour by making her first public speech. She proclaimed: "How proud I am to be Princess of such a wonderful place, and of the Welsh, who are very special to me." The tour had been a resounding personal success for her.

On the last day she and Prince Charles had visited the maternity hospital at Llwynypia in the Rhondda Valley. They had both asked many questions of the new mothers. But the Princess had merely smiled when asked if she and the Prince would be starting a family soon.

In fact she was already pregnant, but this was not made public until November 5. The announcement read: 'The Princess of Wales is expecting a baby next June . . . The Prince and Princess of Wales, the Queen and the Duke of Edinburgh are delighted by the news . . . The Princess is in excellent health.'

The news was received everywhere with great joy.

During the coming months the Princess had to reluctantly cancel several public engagements as she was feeling unwell. She did, however, accompany Prince Charles on a visit to York and Chesterfield. Whilst on 'walkabout' the parents-to-be were showered with hundreds of cuddly toys and baby clothes by well-wishers.

Early in December Diana undertook her first solo engagement when she switched on the Christmas lights in London's Regent Street. The cheers that echoed all along that famous street of elegant shops confirmed that the Princess of Wales was here to stay in her own right.

The new Princess of Wales visits Caernarfon on her first royal tour. She is wearing red and green, the Welsh national colours.

s Christmas 1981 approached, the Prince and Princess went to the Royal Opera House to see a performance of the ballet *Romeo and Juliet*, given in honour of their marriage.

The Princess also visited the St. Mary's junior school in Tetbury, near her home at Highgrove House. She stayed for two hours, joining in the morning assembly and singing carols with the children.

Christmas was spent at Windsor Castle with the Royal Family. Then the Prince and Princess travelled to Sandringham to prepare for the New Year that lay ahead.

In February they took a short break at the secluded resort of Eleuthera in the Bahamas. Unfortunately this trip was marred by the prying lens of a photographer. Subsequently a picture of the Princess wearing a bikini appeared in newspapers and magazines all over the world, earning a sharp reprimand from the Palace for certain Fleet Street newspapers.

Despite this momentary setback the royal couple returned to England looking fit and relaxed.

There were several official engagements to fulfil during the middle months of the Princess's pregnancy, including a charity preview of the West End play *Little Foxes* starring Elizabeth Taylor, and trips to Leeds, Liverpool and Newcastle. Whilst on 'walkabout' in Newcastle the Prince and Princess had suddenly to go to the aid of a small boy trapped in the crush barriers by the surging, excited crowd.

As the weeks and months went by, speculation and

Below: *The proud parents leave St. Mary's hospital with Prince William.*
Below, right: *Prince William of Wales goes on a 'walkabout' of his very own.*

excitement about the forthcoming baby became the nation's chief news story along with details of the Falklands conflict in which Diana's brother-in-law Prince Andrew was serving on board HMS *Invincible*. When asked whether she wanted a boy or a girl, the Princess replied that she didn't mind which so long as the child was healthy.

Eventually she was unable to undertake any more public duties. Shortly after 4.30 a.m. on June 21 1982 Prince Charles drove Diana through the deserted early morning streets of London, to St. Mary's hospital in Paddington. Here, a private room awaited her on the 4th floor of the Lindo Wing.

Some sixteen hours later, at 9.03 p.m. the new baby entered the world, weighing a very healthy 7 pounds 1½ ounces.

Prince Charles who had been present at the birth was "relieved . . . delighted . . . overwhelmed." A few days later he would confess to being "incredibly proud and somewhat amazed."

A notice was posted outside the gates of Buckingham Palace, simply stating that: 'Her Royal Highness The Princess of Wales was safely delivered of a son at 9.03 tonight. Her

Royal Highness and child are both doing well.'

At 11.00 p.m. a beaming Prince Charles stepped out of the hospital to the rousing cheers of the crowd gathered there. Ever since the news had been released they had been singing and chanting and calling for him. Hundreds of questions were fired at him, including "What's his name going to be?" to which the Prince good-naturedly replied "You'd better ask my wife. We've thought of one or two. We've had a little argument about that. We'll find one eventually."

Next day Prince Charles returned to St. Mary's. He was followed by proud family members including the Queen, Earl Spencer, Mrs Shand Kydd and Diana's sisters.

Later that day, and much to everyone's surprise, the Princess and her son left the hospital. The crowd gasped with excitement when Prince Charles emerged from the doorway, his radiant and happy wife by his side, and his son cradled in his arms.

The "argument" about the naming of the child was quickly resolved. He was to be called William Arthur Philip Louis, henceforth to be known as Prince William of Wales: "without any foreshortening in any way" warned the Palace.

The young Prince was christened on August 4 1982, by the Archbishop of Canterbury in the Music Room at Buckingham Palace. The baby was very well-behaved throughout the ceremony, but during the official photo-session afterwards he cried loudly

and everyone agreed with Prince Charles that he'd "got a very good pair of lungs!"

At two months-old Prince William was flown to Balmoral on the same flight as Prince Charles, thereby breaking a royal 'rule' which says that the 1st and 2nd in line to the throne should *not* fly in the same aircraft together.

Seven months later, in March 1983, the young Prince was airborne yet again. This time he was en route to Australia to join his parents who were touring there. The flight was made at the insistence of the Princess who could not bear to be parted from her son while he was so young. Needless to say, the reunion was a joyous occasion.

On February 14 1984 Buckingham Palace announced that the Princess of Wales was expecting her second child. This time she continued to carry out her official duties until the beginning of July.

On the morning of 15th September the Princess was once again admitted to the Lindo Wing of St. Mary's hospital where she occupied the same room as she had during her previous confinement.

His Royal Highness Prince Henry Charles Albert David entered the world at 4.20 p.m., weighing in at 6 pounds 14 ounces.

The news was released half an hour later, and once again the well-wishers gathered outside cheered

Prince William was taken home to Kensington Palace by his nanny, Barbara Barnes.

Just after 2.30 p.m. the royal couple left St. Mary's. The Princess was carrying the new baby in her arms, a tiny bundle wrapped in a white shawl. So radiant did she look that one newspaper called her 'the picture of ideal motherhood'.

Being second and third in line to the throne Prince William and Prince Henry are naturally subjects of great interest to press and public alike. Wisely, though, the royal couple have opted to keep the young Princes away from the public gaze as much as they possibly can during their early years.

There are exceptions, however, such as the day that Prince William started school, and the day when the famous 'Red Devils' parachute team 'dropped in' on Kensington Palace Gardens much to the obvious delight of Prince William. Then there was the celebrated TV programme *In Person: The Prince and Princess of Wales*, presented by Alastair Burnet of ITN, in which the young Princes 'played' piano together inside their Kensington Palace apartment.

For the rest of the time the two boys enjoy all the love and affection that any normal family would lavish on its children. They will also be learning those obligatory 'royal lessons' which will acclimatise them to the lifestyle of protocol, adoration and fame which lays ahead of them both. For theirs is a special place in the world's best-known family.

with joy. Two hours later Prince Charles left the hospital. "We've almost got a full polo team now," he joked.

At 9.00 a.m. next day he returned hand-in-hand with Prince William who had come to see his baby brother for the first time. A short while later a slightly bemused

The Princess of Wales~

At Home & Abroad

he Princess of Wales travels many thousands of miles in a year, both in Britain and around the world. Usually she will be accompanying her husband, but she makes many 'solo' appearances too.

One thing is for sure — her diary is always full.

Wherever she goes she is loved by all, young and old alike. She is always natural, warm and charming no matter where she is or who she is talking to. She also possesses a wonderfully spontaneous sense of humour and is quick to see the funny side of things. It is precisely these qualities which have helped endear her to millions of 'fans' everywhere.

But, as the world also knows, there is a more serious side to the Princess of Wales. She is a caring Princess who patronises many worthy causes.

Particularly close to her heart are organisations devoted to the care of sick and handicapped children. So involved has she become with this aspect of her work that she has learned basic sign language so she can communicate with deaf children.

She is also closely involved with the hospice movement. Indeed, a visit by her to one of those sad establishments does wonders for the morale of the patients.

Other causes close to her heart are various schemes for the relief of urban distress, and the fight against drug abuse.

The Prince and Princess supported the 1985 Band Aid project for famine relief in Africa, and they were quickly on hand to give support and comfort to the victims of the tragedies at Bradford City football ground and at Manchester airport in 1985.

Like all members of the Royal Family the Princess receives many hundreds of invitations each year, from various bodies and organisations requesting her presence at this or that function.

All invitations are carefully sifted by the Princess and her private secretary, and those she chooses to fulfil are fitted into a hectic schedule, often combining two or more visits in the same area.

Once an invitation is accepted, a timetable is carefully worked out to the minutest detail by the Princess's equerry, and she does her homework by reading up about the place she is about to visit.

Meanwhile the city, town or village in question will be subjected to the strictest security checks by the local police force. A 'royal route' will be designated, ready to be cordoned-off on the day of the visit. Menus will have been proposed, checked and approved for the royal meal — usually a buffet luncheon. And the local people will be working themselves into a frenzy of 'royal fever'.

On the great day everyone for miles around will converge on the area of the Princess's visit. Perhaps a 'walkabout' will have been arranged, and all the choicest places along its route will have been nabbed by knowing locals.

The usual army of press photographers will be on the spot too, along with TV film crews and other media people. For, wherever she goes, the Princess is news.

She will travel to the venue either by royal car, train or helicopter, depending on its distance from her homes in London or Gloucestershire.

She will be accompanied by an unobtrusive retinue, each of whom are essential to the smooth running of her visit. This includes one of four ladies-in-waiting, who will walk a few paces behind the Princess ready to help her whenever necessary. The lady-in-waiting always carries a handbag containing certain essential pieces

Below: Diana tries her hand at driving a tank in Berlin.
Right: The Princess is taken for a toy car ride at
Shepparton in Australia.

of equipment — such as scissors and sewing materials, in case of emergency. She will also carry a copy of the royal timetable and of any speeches that the Princess is due to make. (The four ladies-in-waiting work on a rota basis. They provide support and companionship to the Princess and also deal with the mountain of mail sent to her every day.)

Also close at hand will be the Princess's personal detective. He is in constant contact with the local police and keeps a wary eye on the crowd for any signs of trouble or danger.

Apart from visits to various towns and cities, other royal engagements in Britain include things like award ceremonies, charity film premieres, pop concerts and other show-biz events. Another keen interest, which the Princess shares with her husband, is classical music and opera.

Each year sees several royal visits to distant lands, and the Prince and Princess of Wales undertake their fair share of them.

Indeed, this elegant young couple make

the finest ambassadors that Great Britain could wish for. A visit by them greatly increases interest in the United Kingdom and it can do wonders for the British export drive.

Since the royal wedding in July 1981, the Prince and Princess of Wales have, between them, visited Australia, Austria, Canada, Egypt, Hawaii, Italy, Japan, Monaco, New Zealand, Norway, the United States of America, and West Germany.

Naturally, overseas tours require even more planning and organisation than do visits within the British Isles — often arrangements are made a year or more in advance of the visit. The usual retinue of private secretaries, equerries, ladies-in-waiting, private detectives and so on will accompany the royal couple. In addition, a baggage-master is appointed to oversee the 200-300 separate pieces of luggage necessary for such a trip.

But, wherever the royal couple go, the people of all nations clamour to see the Princess of Wales.

Children's Favourite

The Princess of Wales has always retained her love of children everywhere. And in return, children everywhere love her. This wide-eyed little girl presented the Princess with a posy of flowers during her visit to Nottingham. She was rewarded with a kiss — a memory that she will treasure for ever.

This little Irish girl received some royal help to blow out some birthday candles at Dr. Barnardo's home near Stormont in Northern Ireland.

The Princess's Homes

Kensington Palace

When in London the Prince and Princess of Wales live with Prince William and Prince Henry in a luxurious apartment inside *Kensington Palace*. Their home here has three reception rooms, a dining room, three bedrooms, a nursery and quarters for the staff.

Other Royal Family members resident at Kensington Palace are Princess Margaret, Prince and Princess Michael of Kent, the Duke and Duchess of Gloucester and Princess Alice.

Highgrove House

Highgrove House, near Tetbury in Gloucestershire, is the country home of the Prince and Princess of Wales. Prince Charles purchased this magnificent Georgian house in 1980 for a price reportedly in the region of £800,000. Highgrove has nine bedrooms, six bathrooms, a dining room, library, study, and a nursery wing for Prince William and Prince Henry.

There is also a heated swimming pool and an estate of almost 350 acres. The wrought iron gates at the main entrance were given as a wedding present by the local people. The Prince and Princess often spend weekends at Highgrove.

Nearby is Gatcombe Park, the home of Princess Anne and Captain Mark Phillips.

'Tamarisk'

'Tamarisk' is a delightful three-bedroomed bungalow owned by the Prince of Wales. It stands on St. Mary's in the Scilly Isles and provides an ideal retreat from the hurly-burly of royal life.

A fleet of five state Rolls-Royces — *together with several other luxurious limousines — is garaged and maintained in the Royal Mews at Buckingham Palace.*

The livery of each Rolls-Royce is painted in a 'royal claret', so dark it appears to be black. When 'on duty' each car will bear the coat-of-arms of its royal passenger.

Also kept in the Royal Mews are some of the splendid ceremonial coaches *together with the thirty or so horses which are used to pull them through the streets of London on state occasions.*

The Royal Train, *used for distant journeys within Britain, usually has three coaches containing luxury apartments, a kitchen and a dining room.*

For security reasons the train rarely stops at normal British Rail stations — the royal passengers usually disembark at lonely sidings and are transported to their destination by royal car.

When not in commission the Royal Train is kept at a siding in north Buckinghamshire.

The Queen's Flight *is based at RAF Benson in Oxfordshire. It is often used by members of the Royal Family.*

The Flight consists of three turbo-prop Andovers, one Bassett communications' plane and two helicopters. (*Extensive modernisation of The Flight is currently under way and includes the introduction of two British Aerospace 146 Jets.*)

These aircraft are all distinctively marked in red, white and blue. Prince Charles and Prince Philip, both qualified pilots, *often fly themselves to royal engagements.*

The 5769 ton royal yacht HMY Britannia *was launched in April 1953. She is used whenever possible for royal tours overseas.*

Britannia *is manned by twenty-one officers and 256 men of the Royal Navy, each of whom is hand-picked to serve on board. She is the world's largest private yacht and has been described as a 'floating palace' — indeed she is as luxuriously fitted as a stately home.*

'Off Duty'

'Off duty' the Princess of Wales likes to switch-off from the pressures of her hectic schedule by watching TV, reading novels — mostly romantic ones, or listening to tapes of her favourite rock bands.

The Princess has also retained her love of dance, and she goes to the ballet as often as she can.

She has kept up with her own dancing too, and at Christmas-time 1985 was confident enough in her own ability to put on a surprise performance for Prince Charles in partnership with top dancer Wayne Sleep. By all accounts she gave a very polished performance, to the tune of Billy Joel's 'Uptown Girl'.

The Princess of Fashion

efore her engagement to Prince Charles, Lady Diana Spencer was happiest when wearing nothing more elaborate than jeans and sweaters. Indeed, it could be said that the only remarkable thing about her clothes were their very ordinariness, and that the only garments which showed the slightest hint of her future flair were her skiing outfits.

Then, after the announcement of the engagement in February 1981, an astonishing transformation took place.

At that time much was written in the press about the sheer *amount* of clothes being bought from certain fashionable London stores by the Princess-to-be. But of course, as she has since explained, she simply *did not have* the extensive wardrobe necessary for her future lifestyle. All those shopping sprees were both essential and practical.

An early indicator of the power of the Princess over the fashion world came with the appearance of the famous 'Emanuel' wedding dress on the steps of St. Paul's Cathedral. Copies of that

dress were on sale in certain shops within five hours of its public debut.

Today the Princess of Wales retains her position at the forefront of British fashion. For someone who has said that "clothes are not my priority" this is a remarkable position indeed. It seems that everything she wears influences the 'look' of girls everywhere.

At 5 feet 10 inches tall, with long legs and a slim figure, the Princess could easily grace the 'catwalk' of any fashion show.

She is in fact very figure-conscious and keeps in trim by taking regular exercise in the form of swimming and dancing.

She also watches what she eats. She rarely indulges in breakfast, and takes her tea without milk or sugar. On public engagements there is usually a sumptuous feast on offer, but the Princess will resist this temptation. In all likelihood she will choose to nibble at a simple salad, or as she has said to "chase a bit of chicken around the plate".

She has been called 'a living breathing advertisement for the whole of the British fashion trade'. Certainly when she is on an

Right: *A stunning white beaded bare shoulder sheath dress by Hachi.* Centre: *Silk suit in rose pink and white, by the Chelsea Design Company.* Far, right: *Diana always looks stunning in a ski-suit.*

overseas tour, an enormous amount of interest is shown in her British designed clothes, often resulting in large orders for their creators. "If only we could patent her," enthused one British fashion chief.

Among the designers who have benefited from the Princess's patronage are the Emanuels, of course, Joseph Conran, Gina Fratini, Jan Vanvelden, Benny Ong, Bruce Oldfield, Caroline Charles, Hachi, Arabella Pollen and the house of Belville Sassoon.

These days the Princess plays a large part in the design of her clothes. She will often make a drawing of her own ideas and then hand it to the fashion house of her choice. These ideas have often been praised for their professionalism.

All her clothes have to be more than merely 'fashionable', they have to be *practical* too. She calls them "clothes for the job", and will wear a particular garment up to half a dozen times on public engagements.

The pictures on the following pages show just a few of the stunning outfits worn by the Princess of Wales — the Princess of Fashion . . .

Hats...

The sale of hats in Great Britain alone has risen phenomenally since the arrival of the Princess on the fashion scene. She is "good news for the hat trade," said one leading designer. Here are some contrasting examples of royal headgear . . .

...and Hairstyles

The 'Princess Di' hairstyle is still the most popular around. These pictures show some of the variations — as worn by the original . . .

The Glittering Princess

The Princess of Wales is perhaps at her most regal when wearing some of the splendid jewellery borrowed from the Royal Collection. When Prince Charles ascends to the throne, his wife will inherit this fabulous array of tiaras, necklaces and brooches.
The Princess has also begun a fine gems collection of her own.
Here are just a few items of jewellery seen adorning the Glittering Princess . . .

Left: The Princess in knotted pearls at the premiere of the film *Back to the Future.* She is speaking to the master movie maker Steven Spielberg. *Top, right:* A choker necklace studded with diamonds and sapphires. *Top, far right:* The Spencer family tiara, worn by Diana on her wedding day. *Right:* The Queen Mary diamond and pearl drop tiara.

The Princess & Polo

It has often been said that the Princess of Wales is none too keen on polo — her husband's favourite sport!

This stems from the fact that a few days before her wedding she was seen to burst into tears and run away during a polo match. Although this outburst had more to do with a bout of pre-wedding nerves than any dislike of polo, the incident was blown out of all proportion by the press.

Polo is of course a dangerous pastime, as Prince Charles has often discovered when finding himself rather inelegantly dismounted during a game.

In fact the Princess has stated that she enjoys watching the game.

She certainly looks happy enough here. The Prince's team won both matches, incidentally!

The Family Tree of
The Prince & Princess of Wales

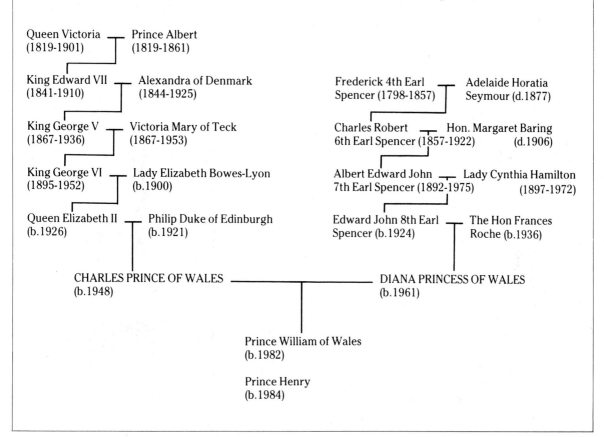

Queen Victoria ___ Prince Albert
(1819-1901) (1819-1861)

King Edward VII ___ Alexandra of Denmark
(1841-1910) (1844-1925)

King George V ___ Victoria Mary of Teck
(1867-1936) (1867-1953)

King George VI ___ Lady Elizabeth Bowes-Lyon
(1895-1952) (b.1900)

Queen Elizabeth II ___ Philip Duke of Edinburgh
(b.1926) (b.1921)

Frederick 4th Earl ___ Adelaide Horatia
Spencer (1798-1857) Seymour (d.1877)

Charles Robert ___ Hon. Margaret Baring
6th Earl Spencer (1857-1922) (d.1906)

Albert Edward John ___ Lady Cynthia Hamilton
7th Earl Spencer (1892-1975) (1897-1972)

Edward John 8th Earl ___ The Hon Frances
Spencer (b.1924) Roche (b.1936)

CHARLES PRINCE OF WALES _____ DIANA PRINCESS OF WALES
(b.1948) (b.1961)

Prince William of Wales
(b.1982)

Prince Henry
(b.1984)

The Kings & Queens of England since 1066

William I (The Conqueror)	1066-1087	Lady Jane Grey	1553
William II	1087-1100	Mary	1553-1558
Henry I	1100-1135	Elizabeth I	1558-1603
Stephen	1135-1154	James I	1603-1625
Henry II	1154-1189	Charles I	1625-1649
Richard I	1189-1199	(Commonwealth	1649-1660)
John	1199-1216	Charles II	1660-1685
Henry III	1216-1272	James II	1685-1688
Edward I	1272-1307	William III and Mary	1689-1702
Edward II	1307-1327	Anne	1702-1714
Edward III	1327-1377	George I	1714-1727
Richard II	1377-1399	George II	1727-1760
Henry IV	1399-1413	George III	1760-1820
Henry V	1413-1422	George IV	1820-1830
Henry VI	1422-1461	William IV	1830-1837
Edward IV	1461-1483	Victoria	1837-1901
Edward V	1483	Edward VII	1901-1910
Richard III	1483-1485	George V	1910-1936
Henry VII	1485-1509	Edward VIII	1936
Henry VIII	1509-1547	George VI	1936-1952
Edward VI	1547-1553	Elizabeth II	1952-

On The Royal Road with Jayne Fincher

The young lady pictured here with cameras around her neck and a small stepladder in her hand is Jayne Fincher. Jayne is a professional photographer who spends most of her working life on the trail of the Royal Family.

Her pictures appear in newspapers and magazines all over the world. Jayne is considered one of today's top royalty watchers, and she has won many awards for her photography.

Her first published picture was a fine study of Prince Charles and his polo pony,

taken at Windsor. "I was really chuffed when I saw that shot used quite big in a national newspaper," remembers Jayne.

Since then she hasn't looked back. She has covered numerous royal tours — including one particularly memorable skiing trip to Klosters in Switzerland when, in pursuit of Prince Charles, she fell and broke her leg.

Jayne was taken to hospital by a mountain rescue unit and later received a note wishing her a speedy recovery from Prince Charles himself. "That really cheered me up," she says. "I'll always treasure that note."

Jayne Fincher has followed the Princess of Wales story ever since those first rumours of the royal romance in 1980. She recalls waiting for hours outside the flat in Coleherne Court where the then Lady Diana Spencer lived. "I didn't particularly like doing it," says Jayne. "The public often picked on us. 'Leave her alone' they'd say and things like that. I often pulled my collar up around my ears,

hoping they'd think I was a man.

"But 'doorstepping' is part of the job of being a photographer. It's something you have to put up with — and I'm quite used to it now."

Jayne remembers the royal wedding with affection — she covered it from a balcony opposite St. Paul's Cathedral — and she brought back some of the best pictures of the honeymoon trip. Since then she has hardly missed a royal event involving the Princess.

A photographer's life on the

'royal road' sounds like a glamorous existence. In fact, it is very hard work indeed. The average weight of cameras, lenses, flashguns, films, filters and other bits and pieces of photographic equipment, is well over 30lbs. This has to be carried around everywhere — especially hard when the royals go on 'walkabout'.

And what of that stepladder? "Most press photographers carry one," explains Jayne. "It's often the only way of securing a good view above the heads of the crowd!"

The Prince and Princess of Wales are among Jayne's favourite royal subjects. "I love photographing Prince Charles in his uniforms or polo outfits. I think he is far more attractive than either of his brothers.

"Princess Diana moves around very quickly — which makes it very difficult to get a sharp picture of her. The best photos of her are those in tight close-up — she has such beautiful eyes. I always try to take pictures which make her look as pretty as she is in real life."

Jayne Fincher took most of the photographs in this *Grandreams Special.*